# GET PAID UPFRONT TO WRITE YOUR BOOK

Insider Secrets from Chris O'Byrne, President of JETLAUNCH.net, the Super-Fast Book Design Company

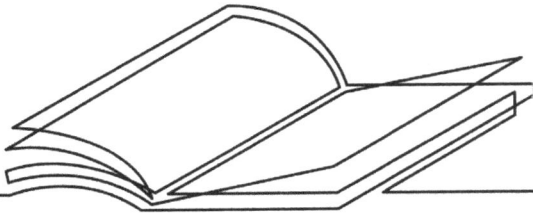

## CHRIS O'BYRNE

ISBN: 978-1-64184-033-0 (paperback)
ISBN: 978-1-64184-034-7 (ebook)

# TABLE OF CONTENTS

# AUTHOR'S NOTE

Getting paid to write a book is something we usually think is reserved for well-known authors with traditional publishers who land an advance on their royalties, giving them some living expenses while they hide in a room and type away for hours every day trying to meet a deadline.

You're going to learn how you can get paid upfront to write your book, earn far more than any advance you might get with a traditional publisher, and even start a new career or a very profitable extra income stream.

# IF YOU'RE A SPEAKER

Most speakers start their speaking career by talking about whatever topics they feel that they have expertise in. Then, somewhere down the line, they think, "You know, if I had a book, I could sell it from stage and earn more money. It would also help me get more speaking gigs. It would make me look better." And then they sit down to try to write a book, which they find is a very long and arduous task for most people.

What they don't realize is that the talks they are giving have already written the book for them. All they need to do is record their talks, have them transcribed and turned into books or booklets that they can sell at events or online through Amazon or with a free plus shipping funnel, and get far more speaking gigs as a result, build their brand, and explode their business.

Speakers put a lot of time and effort into writing and delivering their talks. They usually have several talks already planned, practiced and ready to go, and they sell those to companies or organizations that hire people to come and speak. This might be bigger businesses. It could be a small business. It could be a college. It could be a church. It could be a non-profit organization. It just depends on your market is and how you market yourself. Those talks that they have spent so much time polishing and perfecting are completely ready to turn into their book. If they have several talks all around a common theme, which is usually the case, all of those could be recorded and transcribed and turned into a full-length book. Be sure to always video record your speaking engagements!

The other method that I recommend is to turn each talk into a highly potent booklet. Each one of those booklets can become excellent lead generation devices, and they can be condensed or combined into one larger book after the booklets have been out for a while and have done their thing to bring in more business.

Make sure you also have time for people to ask questions because those questions will give you even more ideas to write and talk about. It's like doing an "ask" campaign where you find out where people's biggest struggles are, what they are grappling with, and what they need the most help with, and then you provide that help for them. Later, I'll teach you how to take that video and use it to jetlaunch your entire career or your business or your brand or whatever it is that you are trying to build.

Experienced speakers have a big advantage because they already have their material written and perfected and practiced, so all they have to do is record the speech or the talk that they give. It's a very simple, and relatively easy and inexpensive process at this point to create a book or a series of booklets. Every single one of those—along with all of the extra marketing materials that you will learn how to create and use from your recorded video—are solid gold.

## If You're Already Teaching

Some of you are already teachers. You're teaching a course. You're teaching a class. You're getting in front of people in some way, either live or online, and you are teaching valuable information. All of that information, those courses, the things that you are already doing, are material for your book. You've already done the work, now you just need to turn it into a book. The same could be said for any blog posts that you've written, any videos that you've recorded, or Instagram, Facebook, YouTube, et cetera. Any material that you have presented in any way on any platform is just waiting for you to use to write and publish your book. In fact, many of you have enough material for many booklets, even many books, you just need to put in the effort of getting it turned into book form.

# IF YOU HAVE NO CONTENT

Now, let's go to the other end of the spectrum, the person who has no content out there. They haven't written anything. They haven't recorded anything. They may not have any idea of what to talk about. They have a business or they're trying to start a business, and it might be a product business, a service business, or an info product business. Whatever it is, the effort that you put in to teaching your material, recording that, and turning it into a book, is going to be extremely valuable. Not only are you creating valuable marketing materials, but you're also establishing yourself as an expert and creating, in the form of a book or booklets, the most effective content and content marketing machine possible.

Let's use me as an example. I have been running a book design business for many years, and we've done very well and have grown significantly in the last four years, each year growing faster and faster. I've done a little bit of writing, but hardly any. I've done a little bit of video, but again, hardly any. So I don't have any material ready to turn into a book or booklets. However, I have a lot of knowledge about the book industry, especially self-publishing and book marketing and using your book or booklets to build your brand and your business. That knowledge is just waiting for me to get it out in some form that will be turned into a book and booklets.

My first booklet, which I just got done designing and getting printed, was created from an interview that someone did with me via Facebook Live. It was about 45 minutes long, and I took that material, had it tran-scribed, edited it myself (because I am a professional editor) had it designed by my company, and—boom—I have a booklet.

For my next booklets, including this one, I wrote a list of several topics in which I know that I have expertise and have talked to other people about informally, on the phone or via email. I know that I could talk more about these topics because there's a lot of infor-mation just sitting in my head, waiting to be put down into audio or written form so I can turn it into a book.

Just this morning, on a long drive I'm taking to a mastermind event that I am speaking at, I wrote, via voice recording, a book about the free plus shipping method for selling tons of books. That has already been sent in to be transcribed, and then I will edit it and turn that into another booklet. The talk that I'm giving this weekend will be turned into another booklet. That means that, not only am I writing three booklets in one week, but today I wrote two booklets as I drove, simply by recording myself and having them transcribed.

At this rate, I could easily write one book a day for several days in a row. How easy would it be for you to write a list of all of the topics that you already know a lot about, that you're already an expert at, and then turn each one of those into a booklet? In one year's time, you could have over 50 booklets, and most of those could then be combined into full-length books. If it took 10 booklets to create one book, that means that in one year's time you would have written five full-length books. It is amazing how productive you can be when you know the right techniques and when you leverage the work of other people.

In my case, I'm leveraging the work of **JETLAUNCH.net**, my own company, to design the books for me. I will then hire someone, again within my own company, to do Amazon ads and get traction on Amazon that way, and then also hire someone to create a book funnel for me. I will have a book funnel for each of these booklets. My upsell would be the recorded audio, or the video if I recorded video for it, and I could also use other booklets that I've written as additional upsells and cross-sells and sell them in a buddle. There is no limit to what you can do with this.

# GET PAID TO TEACH

However, this booklet is about how to get paid upfront to write your booklet. Instead of merely recording myself talking through this book, the next step is to create a course or a series of courses that I will teach live, in person, in various cities, and I will also teach as an online course. I will also create a group coaching program based on all of the material that I am creating and recording and turning into booklets. That coaching program, of course, is not me getting paid upfront, but it is a valuable way for me to get paid after the fact, many times more than I could ever get paid as a well-known author with a traditional publishing company earning maybe 8% royalties.

The first step to getting paid to write your book is to create a course series that you will teach. First, come up with a list of seven to ten topics that you can spend about an hour talking about. You will then have another hour for question and answers so that you can get even more material for your book. This Q&A is like having a live "ask" campaign where you find out what people either don't understand about what you're teaching, or they ask about some facet that you had not even thought about. You also find out what they're actually struggling with, so you can learn their pain points and provide a solution. Some of those ideas will turn into new courses and books.

Each one of those topics will become a chapter in your book, or you could turn each topic into a separate booklet first and then combine them in a few months into a new, full-length book. Once you have planned out the names of each chapter, the topics for each talk, you then want to create an outline for each one of those.

Now, I know from experience that that hour can go by pretty quickly, especially when you're talking about something you know a lot about. It helps to have it planned out ahead of time and to practice talking about it. You can keep a list in front of you of your main talking points, and include stories, anecdotes, and examples because story selling works well.

Please don't feel like you need to get your presentation down perfect. You're teaching a class; it will be interactive. It's okay to stumble or stutter or to say "um" a lot. Yes, you want to practice so you can improve, but when you first start out, I give you permission to make a complete and utter fool of yourself while you are teaching. I used to teach high school, and my first year was terrible! Realize that you could look terrible, and people will still get a lot of value out of what you are teaching them, so relax. Learn to enjoy the experience.

Think of it as you are talking to one of your children and teaching them or you're teaching a friend. Be casual and conversational. When you are talking with a friend, you're not worried about how you sound or if you're covering every topic exactly right. None of that matters or makes a difference. You are going to do just fine being yourself, having a list of things to talk about and stories to tell so that you don't forget. Yes, practice a few times so that you do feel somewhat comfortable, but don't get it to the point of perfection. Don't get it to the point where you are repeating a speech word for word. You're not giving a presentation; you are teaching people. That process is more one-on-one with each person in the room, each person that you're talking to. It's much more casual and conversational.

The next step is to choose when and where you are going to give your classes. I do recommend, if possible, that you give your classes live, in person, because a live workshop, even if it's just a two-hour workshop, is going to carry a lot more weight. It's going to be a lot more valuable to someone, so they are going to be willing to pay you $100 or $200 to come to hear you talk. The more your potential customer values what you teach them, the more that you can charge.

You also, of course, want to video record the entire thing. Do you need fancy equipment? Should you spend thousands of dollars on lighting and cameras and recording and microphones? No. This process can be very simple. I use my iPhone to video record. I also have a remote microphone, which cost me, I don't know, maybe $70, and that remote mic makes it so that I don't have to worry about where I place the phone. I don't have to be close to it so that it picks up my voice.

As you walk back and forth, the remote mic will pick up everything much better than if you try to get your phone way up close and in front of people. It'll be intrusive and annoying, and it will be a lot less natural because you'll be focusing on placing yourself in front of that microphone. Of course, you could still set things up that way. You could use a camcorder with a boom mic. You can go all the way up to fancier stuff if you want, but even as you get into the fancier stuff, you're not going to spend a whole lot of money.

You also have to figure out where you will teach your courses, classes, or workshops. You have many options for a venue. Some people have a large home and can invite people into their house. If you have a smaller group, you might find that your living room or dining room is large enough. You can also rent a conference room or even bigger. It depends on how many people you want to attend. You can also rent a room at a hotel, and I don't mean rooms where you sleep. Most hotels have conference rooms and places where people can have meetings or give talks or presentations.

Many libraries have private rooms, and there are also companies that rent rooms. For example, in my town, the electric utility company rents rooms for a very low cost. All you have to do is call and ask or do a search on Google or Facebook. Be a little creative and do a little research, and you'll find plenty of potential venues for your class. Personally, especially when I'm traveling, I like to give talks at hotels. I can also get a room to spend the night, and it makes the whole thing nice and easy. And if you're going to fly to another city, you can rent a room at a hotel near the airport, so you don't even have to rent a car.

Another idea is to rent an Airbnb house. Rent a large house via Airbnb, someplace that you probably would never stay because it's large enough to be a mansion. There many of those that you can rent for a fairly decent price if they are big places where you can have people come in and listen to you and spend two hours or longer.

You now have your series of talks planned out. You have your location figured out. You have your equipment figured out. You're pretty much done at this point. You've done the hardest work. All you have to do now is give your talks, record them, have them transcribed, and turn it into a book.

And this is where it starts to get fun. This is where you can get a lot more traction out of your book and create your very own MMM or Massive Marketing Machine.

# HOW MUCH CAN YOU GET PAID?

Let's dig into how much you can get paid to give these talks because, after all, that's the main point of this booklet!

Let's say that you charge $100 for a two-hour session. People will pay that because they want to learn something that's very valuable to them. Let's say you get 30 people to attend. If you get 30 people paying $100 each, that's $3,000 per class that you teach.

However, if you teach 10 classes, that is $30,000 that you get paid—upfront—to actually write your book. $30,000 will easily cover everything you need to spend to get your video professionally edited, turned into a book, and selling. Once you start teaching these classes, however, you may find that you enjoy the process; you don't have to go through this just once.

You can teach these courses over and over again. You can even do it without traveling much if you go to local or regional cities. Most people live fairly close, within two to three hours, of some bigger cities, and I'm talking a population of 100,000 or more, cities that are big enough for you to get a decent number of people to come to your presentation.

If you do that, let's say that you now teach this course 10 times in a year, you are now earning $300,000, which is a significant income, and you are doing relatively little work because once you have your talk planned out, all you have to do is show up and talk to people.

## Additional ways to earn money

You are also going to make money in a couple of different ways. When you set up your sales page for people to sign up to attend your talk, you will create a sales funnel where you give people the option upfront, before they even come to your talk, to pay extra, maybe $197, to get the video recording of the talk that they will attend. People find great value in that because it's hard to take enough notes, and most people feel they'll miss something. If they can relax the whole time you're speaking, knowing that they can watch that video later on at their leisure, that's of high value to them.

And remember, you already know you'll turn this talk into a booklet. You could also sell the book to them ahead of time. They can pre-order the book for $20 just to be the very first ones to receive it. People love being the first one to get something.

You can also do an upsell of the audiobook version. Because you are recording your talk, you can extract the audio from the edited video and turn that into an audio-book. Another option is to record yourself reading the edited version of your booklet using some decent audio equipment. Not only can you sell your audiobook directly to your customers, but you can also put it up on Amazon/Audible and get more sales and a bigger audience that way. You could also then include another upsell to a coaching program or any other high-ticket offer you might have.

Another offer that you can upsell to is a personal one-on-one session with you. Let's say that my presentation is about how to write a book or a booklet that builds your brand and explodes your business. I know that the people coming are going to be interested in building their brand or their business, so I can upsell them to a one-hour or a two-hour one-on-one session where I sit down with them, look at their business, look at their model and strategies, and come up with ideas for their book or booklets. It's a highly personalized strategy session.

Your strategy session is a session where you can go back and forth with each other, coming up with ideas and digging deeper into the marketing aspects of it, because even though you can talk about the general marketing aspects, it always is much more valuable to talk to somebody one-on-one, helping them figure out the best way to use a book to build their business or brand. That one-on-one talk, by the way, can easily sell for $500 to $2,000, depending on your market and depending on the return that they will see for what you offer.

When you add up all of these different revenue streams, just from the talks that you're giving you are now into the many, many thousands of dollars. And once you start getting into that kind of money, which is really easy to do once you know the path, you are now far ahead of most traditional authors who only get advances on their royalties.

## Personal Example

To show that I follow my own advice, I offer something similar to what I just described. However, my upsell is different, and I want you to see how creative you can be with your offer.

First, my basic offer is a one-day workshop where I teach people how to write and publish a booklet. We start by creating a list of potential topics, then we go into depth about the writing process, including transcription and editing. Next, you learn how the design process works, and then you learn different ways to sell and market your booklet.

My first upsell is to pre-purchase the video recording of the event for $197. My next upsell is a two-hour recording session where we help you teach your booklet content, and we video record the entire session. We then have your video edited, transcribed, and turned into a sellable video, an audiobook, and a booklet. We also create an MMM (Massive Marketing Machine), which we will learn about next.

As an additional upsell, we also offer an Amazon Ad service to sell tons of your books on Amazon, and we create your customized free + shipping funnel to sell even more books, plus build your mailing list and other valuable marketing assets.

# HOW TO CREATE YOUR MMM (MASSIVE MARKETING MACHINE)

The best part of the video recording process is how you are going to use these recordings to create a massive amount of marketing materials that you can use to sell your courses, get people to go to your talks, sell your book, sell your services, and if you own a business—a service or product or even an info product business, a business that is not based on doing these talks and teaching these courses—you will generate some serious leads for that business.

You start by massively repurposing your video. First, as we've already mentioned, you can sell that video as an upsell to people that go to your course, that come to see you talk. You can also split that video into pieces and put those pieces on Instagram, Instagram TV, Facebook, Facebook Live, YouTube, and

LinkedIn. There are many places where you can put your video up, and you could do it in a series of, say, 10-minute clips. If you talk for two hours, for example, you will have 12 clips that you can use. Most video courses that you watch include a series of videos that are each in the range of five to 10 minutes long.

You can then, of course, take that same video material, turn it into a paid course that you can sell through your website, or if you want, you can go through someplace like Udemy, Thinkific, Teachable, etc. There are a lot of places where you can sell online courses.

You can also take photo clips, photo stills from your videos of you presenting. Get some good photos of you actively teaching or explaining something. You can take several stills, adds quotes, and turn those into Instagram posts. Those are very popular and very good at building your Instagram, which of course you can then leverage and use to sell more books and courses and get people onto your mailing lists.

Let me say something quick about professional editing. If you are not going to have your transcribed manuscript professionally edited, you might as well not even do it. If you don't have your booklet professionally edited, you will look bad, and you will lose business. You will hurt your brand instead of building it up. You won't look like the professional that you really are, so please have it professionally edited. It doesn't cost that much, and it is well worth the time and money.

You also have a lot of written material to repurpose. You can split your manuscript into multiple blog posts, many Facebook posts, articles on LinkedIn or even one longer article that you can post on Medium. You can put these clips up all over the place. All of your written material is super valuable.

You now have video. You have photos. You have audio. You have written material. If you are creative, and you put a little bit of thought and effort into this, you'll come up with many more ways that you could use these materials than what I'm giving you here in the limited space that I have.

Now, just by doing these courses and recording them, you have created a Massive Marketing Machine that not only will bring in a lot of money, but it will also jetlaunch your brand and explode your business. You cannot believe how effective it is to have a widespread content marketing system that does your brand and business building for you. This includes not only all of the marketing materials but the booklets and the book itself, in addition to the video and audio recordings you can sell.

# CREATE AN ENTIRELY NEW BUSINESS

All of this combined is enough to, well, it's enough to create a new business! You could drop whatever it is you're doing and do just this and live very comfortably just from this one series of courses. Each year you could create another course, another series of classes that you teach, and repeat the same thing all over again. And maybe you keep doing the first one, and you've got the second, and then maybe you do a third one. You could see how far you can take this and how much you can build your brand and your income.

And remember, this is the exact method that many of the big names have done to build their own brands and businesses, and I'm talking about people like Tony Robbins, Brendon Burchard, Lewis Howes, Gary Vaynerchuk, Grant Cardone, and Ed Mylett. Many people have done this same thing where they leveraged their books, leveraged the materials from creating those books, got paid to create these books in the first place, and then went on to have massive speaking engagements or coaching programs or live events. Look at the events that Tony Robbins does. All of these things were made possible because these authors, authors who started out just like you, put in the effort to come up with something helpful and valuable for people that they felt they had some expertise in.

They weren't experts. They had expertise. They had knowledge. They learned something along the way, and they leveraged by writing books and creating courses. You can become just like any of those big-brand people simply by following this plan, following this method, following this strategy.

# ABOUT THE AUTHOR

A former chemical engineer and high school teacher, Chris O'Byrne built JETLAUNCH.net into the premier book and booklet company for entrepreneurs, speakers, coaches, and consultants.

Chris now teaches people around the world how to write and publish a booklet in one week or less.

Your expert booklet will generate tons of leads and position you as an authority. Build your business; build your brand.

JETLAUNCH.net has been used by successful entrepreneurs and authors like John Lee Dumas, Ed Mylett, James Smiley, Dan Norris, Charlie Gilkey, Rachel Pedersen, Kary Oberbrunner, Dan Sullivan, and members of Lewis Howes' Inner Circle.

Booklets are the hottest thing
in lead generation today!

Want your own expert booklet?

It's easy, and your ROI will be
through the roof.

We will help you:
- Write your booklet
- Edit
- Design (cover, print, and ebook)
- Launch and market
- Done in a few short weeks, not months

Go to:
**jetlaunch.net**

Start your booklet today!